MW01383381

"Billie Williams employees a unique, down-to-earth way of word association to teach writing skills. By using vivid picturesque tricks, her work is designed to help any beginning writer remember the basic rules of storytelling, and how and when to use them." JoEllen Conger, Author

"I just finished reading a delightful little book called 'Writing Wide: Exercises in Creative Writing' by Billie A. Williams. Writers and teachers of writing alike will find this book an invaluable resource. 'Writing Wide' is a short book but it is jam-packed with useful information. The book makes a wonderful addition to any writer's (or writing teacher's) collection." Karen Mueller Bryson, playwright, novelist, and educator

"As the title suggests, WRITING WIDE covers a wide range of ideas for the new writer as well as reminders for those more seasoned. A good book and a good read, chock full of suggestions to inspire any writer's imagination." Peggy P. Parsons w/a Evanell

"Billie Williams' *Writing Wide, Exercises in Creative Writing*, is itself a literal and fun manifestation of creative writing. Williams uses everything from blowing bubblegum through a tooth gap to the late winter sun melting snowy shoeprints, to guide the novice writer through the creative process. Her thought provoking and original imagery will prod you through the teaching text and writing exercises. Enjoy and start writing!" Karen Rinehart, www.KarenReinhart.com

"In Writing Wide, Billie A. Williams writes with clarity, simplicity and wisdom. Each chapter talks to the novice writer and leads her towards action. Williams talks of a writer's words contained by 'the wide picket fence of teeth', of 'marinating the story in your mind', of approaching the first draft with 'mind wide open.'

My advice: Do a quick read of Writing Wide the first time, and then go back to the beginning and indulge yourself." Shery Ma Belle Arrieta, Author http://ewritersplace.com

"Ms. Williams in Writing Wide: Exercises in Creative Writing provides a fascinating primer that can be incorporated into any student's writing program.... The author uses a 'writing wide' motif and vivid colorful images to illustrate 14 imaginative elements (chapters) applicable to writing stories. You will take a significant step towards finding meaning in self-expression, writing, and discovery activities. I highly recommend Writing Wide to you." David L. Johnson, Ph.D.

"I really like Writing Wide -- Williams has a gift for painting pictures that make sense. Your words create mental images that are easy to remember. At the same time they paint a picture on how to paint a better picture with words." Karen Saari Secore, L & K Associates

"Billie Williams's book Writing Wide gives you the tools you need to expand your creative thinking, to see your writing in a new light and then, use that vision to take it to the next level. It's a fun, interactive look at writing and life that provides ideas real people can use every day." Shirley Jump, author

Writing Wide

Exercises in Creative Writing

By

Billie A. Williams

Writing Wide

Exercises in Creative Writing

Billie A Williams

First Edition

Filbert Publishing * Kandiyohi, Minnesota

Writing Wide, Exercises in Creative Writing

Manufactured in the United States of America.

Published by Filbert Publishing, Box 326, Kandiyohi, Mn, 56251, USA.
FilbertPublishing.com

ISBN 0-9710796-3-3

LCCN: 2003110449

Writing Wide

Exercises in Creative Writing

By

Billie A. Williams

Table of Contents

Writing Wide

Compares secret keeping and the effects of a space between your teeth... meaning you can't keep a secret. In addition, this chapter explores how to write while holding your secret, letting the secret loose a little at a time.

Learning all the rules so you can break them to write your own truth and expand your knowledge, imagination, and interpretation of the life around you.

Compares the wide angle lens of a camera shooting a panoramic shot and the panoramic view of your story idea before you pull out to focus on a close up portrait.

This is used for comparison in the choosing of clues to follow your characters in your story, enlarging on their connection to the story.

5. *Wide Mouth* - Jar - Page 27

Compares canning and freezing produce to story design, plotting and fitting it together at the proper moment.

6. *Wide Screen* - Television – Page 30

This chapter explores the wide screen, surround sound, and how to capture your novel or story's with intensely vivid prose.

7. *Wide Berth* - to creativity – Page 34

Letters with tails that flow… the letters with flowing tails are used to give the reader an eye into how to relax and alleviate writer''s block or the work stoppage associated with fatigue.

8. *Wide Trailer* - Double -Wide - Page 38

The double wide trailer or mobile home is used as an example of what your novel or stories parts and pieces are, how they are arranged, and how and where to place them inside the four walls of your story.

9. *Wide Open* Imagination – Page 41

"Wide Open" is how to write your first draft. In this chapter, we compare it to the volcano's eruption, hot molten lava and the cooling of that lava to form rock. Then in that same hard, black lava, we explore the emergence of new green shoots of life from the rock hard soil as it relates to the craft of writing.

10. *Wide Leg* - of the Gray Elephant– Page 45

The fable of the three blind men and the elephant serve as an example of how your reader sees your story if you do not use concrete description, narration and characterization to help them visualize what your story is showing him. It is the writer's job to create a vision for the reader.

11. *Wide Leaf Plant* - Page 49

The Croton is used to compare a story to the total plant. How to feed, grow, and nurture a healthy specimen, be it plant or story.

12. *Wide Shadow* – Page 53

Wide Shadow uses the different intensity of daylight occurring in the morning, at noon and in the afternoon. Light sources are also brushed upon as sunlight; moon glow and artificial light play a part as point of view creators. This section compares writing and point of view to the way shadows are displayed different times of day.

13. *Wide Receiver* – about the synopsis - Page 58

What to include and how to look at your whole picture in terms of what the editor is looking for. It compares the synopsis to a football team and its key players.

14. *Wide Writing* - Corralling the wild stallion. Page 62

Here we examine six ways to tighten up your writing. Comparing it to the horses in a corral, we look at wimpy verbs the nags of the literary world; locoweed prepositions; over weight adverbs; twin horse redundancies; and appaloosa similes and metaphors.

Chapter One

The Wide Space Between Teeth

"It was the secrets of heaven & earth that I desired to learn."

Mary Wollstonecraft Shelley, English Poet

I noticed that he had a wide space between his teeth. Rather like a younger Rip Torn of the television series "Topper". Mother used to say that having a wide space between your teeth meant you could not keep a secret.

As a child, I pictured a fat bubble gum pink secret squirting out from between those wide apart teeth and splatting against the secret receiver's ear. That would effectively plug the receiver's ear and block the message. Secret teased but not given.

Writing is like that. When you write you try to keep the secret of the whole story contained, but it is anxious to ooze out between the barriers and splat against the listener /reader's ear. It dares them to listen harder, dig deeper, pay attention; a secret is about to be revealed. A great pink, sweet, sticky secret is about to be given away.

Our words are contained by the white picket fence rows of teeth, except for that space. We really do want our story to leak out, escape through that gap in a measured fashion. Chapter by chapter, beginning, middle, and end the book leaks onto the page.

Did you ever notice when you chew bubble gum that as the bubble gum is warmed you want, almost have to, blow bubbles? Think about what it is that you do when you blow a bubble. First, you push your tongue into the gum and stretch and try to force it between your teeth all the while you try to hold it back. Then you blow, slowly and carefully. As the bubble grows –you blow slower and eventually pinch it off, before it bursts or deliberately waiting for it to burst.

That is how it is with writing too. All your story's secrets are contained in that bubble. You held them with out letting them explode for your reader, until you were ready. The reader gets the pleasure of seeing the bubble develop as he turns the pages, breath (chapter) by breath (chapter). The bubble (your story) gets bigger and the edges start getting thinner so that the reader begins to see through the bubble to the wide space in those teeth that can't keep a secret.

When enough air (facts or details) have been forced into the bubble (story), it bursts with a loud bang and all the air (details) rush out in the climax of your story. The bubble collapses in on itself (denouement) and the narrator sucks the gum (story) into his mouth to begin yet another story. The reader, meanwhile, has had a sharp surprise. He felt the rush of air and little spatters of gum (story facts) spurt into his face when the story burst full-blown into its finish. Aha! You say.

The narrator, with the wide space between his front teeth, finally told the story''s secret.

EXERCISES:

1.) Write a story pretending you are teaching some one how to blow a bubble. Be sure to have a beginning, middle and end.

2.) Using one of the quotes below as a story starter, write a paragraph about secrets.

QUOTES:

"Journalists belong in the gutter because that is where the ruling classes throw their guilty secrets." Gerald Priestland, English writer & journalist

"For secrets are edged tools, and must be kept from children and from fools." John Dryden, English Poet & Playwright

Chapter Two

Wide Ruled Paper

"The moral life of man forms part of the subject matter of the artist, but the morality of art consists in the perfect use of an imperfect medium."

Oscar Wilde, Anglo-Irish Dramatist & Poet

Wide lines on wide ruled paper is what you used when you first began to write so that you had room to make tall and short letters and still stay between the lines. Then when you mastered the letterform and size, you chose narrow ruled paper to show how controlled and grown-up you were. You were able to follow the rules and stay between the lines so well. Narrow thinking, following all the rules, staying with in the lines.

Then you went back to wide rule paper. While you still wrote narrow rule sized letters, you used wide rule because someone whispered, "Read between the lines". So you wrote your narrow minded, according to the rules, alphabet perfect stories to please the teacher while you secretly wrote the real story between the lines.

The beginning is a nice polite thesis stating your premise in perfect, narrow, between the lines grammar, and sequential thinking.

Dick and Jane were brother and sister. They loved each other. They helped each other with chores every day. Mother was very happy with them. She hugged and kissed them and read them fairy tales at bedtime. Dick fed and cared for his dog Spot. He played with him every day. Jane fed and cared for her cat Puff. She played with her everyday.

Yada yada yada *ad nauseam.*

All the while the story between the lines developed. Bonnie and Clyde hated each other. Clyde hated having to drag his sister Bonnie to school every day. Moreover, he hated getting beat up trying to protect her from the bully she taunted until the bully threatened to kill her.

You present a mediocre middle where you enlarged on the premise. We have Dick and Jane with a new family member all cooing and sweet. Playing patty cake with the new baby Sally and helping mommy with all the chores Dick and Jane fully engage in the nicety of the day. Smiling all the while.

Meantime between the lines Bonnie and Clyde are terrorizing the neighborhood. They found, as a team, they could let modifiers dangle, split infinitives, and even toss in a fragment of a sentence to yell "danger!" or obscenities at the perfect sentence.

Then comes the stark and perfect ending. Dick and Jane, Spot and Puff, Mommy and Daddy and baby Sally live happily every after doing all the nice perfect sentence, perfect grammar, perfect penmanship, between the lines living a family can do.

While between the lines, you do your Martin Short impression of on the wild side. You burst at the seams and scribble maniacally, obliterating the fine lines between good and evil, right and wrong. You dare to write an unhappy ending; you dare to challenge the authority that said that you had to stay between the lines. The grammar was true and good. The sentence structure is terse and bright. The story was aflame with passion for the written words. You wrote between the lines, but in the bigger spaces where the real story lies.

Now you can use plain paper or your computer and have as much or as little white space on the page as you choose. You learned the rules so that you would know how to break them. No one would care, or even notice, because the story grabbed him or her, pulled h/her in, and held them captive until the story said "The End".

EXERCISES:

1.) Rewrite a favorite fairy tale and be sure to change the ending. Find something that needs to be written between the lines as defined above.

2.) Tell a story about a lie either you or someone else told. Tell it as if it was necessary – how much white space you/they needed to surround it with to make it believable.

QUOTES:

"A memory of yesterday's pleasures, a fear of tomorrow's dangers, a straw under my knee, a noise to mine ear, a light in mine eye, an anything, a nothing, a fancy, a chimera in my brain, troubles me in my prayers. So certainly is there nothing, nothing to spiritual things, perfect in this world." John Donne, English Poet

Chapter Three

Wide Angle Lens

"To me, photography is the simultaneous recognition, in a fraction of a second of the significance of an event as well as of a precise organization of forms which give that event its proper expression."

Henri Cartier-Bresson, French Photographer & Artist

When you use a wide-angle lens on a camera, you do so to get a panoramic view of your subject. Why would you want to do that? Shouldn't you focus, center your picture, compose it of close-knit items? As with your writing, some times you need to see the broad picture in order to focus on the single most important element, be it story or picture.

If you were to take a panoramic view of an event in your life and write down everything you can see, feel, or hear in detail, you begin to see what makes up a scene, or the setting, in your writing. As you look at the big picture, you pick and chose details to tell your readers that may be pertinent to understanding your story people and the story itself. However, you need elements from the big picture, the panoramic view, to make the setting feel real. It is these subtle nuances that make a scene come to life.

I recommend that you try this as an exercise with at least five events from your life. Try to make the events as varied as you can; say a happy, sad, fun, loathsome, and perhaps interesting event. Ten would be even better, but you can always add to this list, and you should regularly. It will help you see details. It will help you become more aware of details that set the stage and make it believable. This will help you develop settings with a feel for time and place in your story.

After you have the broad view of your story, you decide where your focus will be. Use the same focus on your protagonist and your supporting characters. Go so far as to do a character sketch of each. By doing this it will help you focus to a single center of your picture. You will need to answer the questions, "What does my main character want?" The rest of the picture composes itself as other characters decide their needs. Each character is deciding what s/he is willing to do to achieve his/her goal.

Think of an extended family portrait, each person is connected to the others some how. So to are your characters in your story. Each character's life touches someone else in your story in a significant way or h/she would not be there. Like the panoramic photograph, all things are connected in some way. Every character some how depends on or needs one of the other characters to fulfill a need or goal of their own.

For instance, think of your protagonist as the main/father/mother figure of the family. S/He is responsible for his/her own actions. Whatever she does however affects the rest of the family/cast of characters.

If she robs a bank, the family is drawn into that. Perhaps the oldest child drives the get-away-car; maybe the aunt provides a hiding place, etc.

Fill out your story with things from your panoramic view of things you know to be true for your story. You could begin with an outline – I know the dreaded word -- outline – but it could be what you need to take each item from the panoramic view of your story and connect them through scene and chapter via the outline. Think of it as a blueprint for stage setting, or the map for treasure, what ever it takes to get you to pick apart your story and make an outline/tree of where the story is going to take you.

Put another way, we could say start your picture from a single portrait – it may be a very fine portrait indeed, but it tells us little of the story behind it. If you were to take that portrait and add his/her favorite chair, a small table, a book, perhaps a piano your character starts to become a person rather than just an image on a piece of canvas. If you start with your center and build a panoramic view – you will have fleshed out your character and in so doing your story.

EXERCISES:

1.) Take a picture of someone from your life, maybe an old school photo of just that person. Write out in detail all you see as you show us who that person is. You cannot add any background that is not in the picture. Would we know your friend or family member if we saw them on the street from the way you described him or her? Does this person have a story to tell based on physical appearance only?

2.) Look at a magazine photo or one of your own that has a panoramic view and tell in vivid detail what it contains so that if some one were blind they could see what you see in their minds eye.

QUOTES:

"*A photograph is a secret about a secret. The more it tells you the less you know.*" Diane Arbus, American Photographer.

"*The photographer is like the cod, which produces a million eggs in order that one may reach maturity*". George Bernard Shaw, Irish Dramatist.

Chapter Four

Wide Shoe Width

"Old friends are best. King James used to call for his old shoes; they were easiest for his feet."

John Selden, English historian & antiquary

A wide shoe leaves a big print in the fresh snow. When the sun shines on it, the print enlarges from the heat. This same thing happens in your story. As the characters march through the story, they leave footprints. As we learn more about each one, they become larger footprints in our mind. It is as though the sun light of our clues begins to enlarge them much as the footprints in the snow. We develop an affinity for the characters. We will either like or dislike them as the author outlines their footprints for us. We follow them through the snowy field of the story judging each one by the marks s/he leaves in the landscape. The protagonist and antagonists footprints will be the largest and become even larger as we turn up the heat on their paths.

Secondary characters in the story will come and go on the story path leaving different footprints. You will notice the landscape change as you move through the pristine snowy field. The presence of all those footprints could muddy the terrain, especially if your story is of the mystery genre. The secondary character's prints are meant to lead you astray. You may need to follow them briefly because they are so similar to your antagonist's. However, you soon discover the tread style is different once they separate from the crowd. As in your story line, you examine other suspects, eliminating them one by one.

Your antagonist will leave a trail throughout your story that the protagonist will sniff out and show the reader. The narrator will declare in the protagonist's voice, "this is the way he went; this is how he did the deed."

The antagonist may try to change shoes, but they will always be wide and the switch will leave clues of the switch. The protagonist is hot on his trial now and will not be lead astray. All the other footprints disappear as the protagonist eliminates their shoe prints and shows us the antagonist's. He shows us that the antagonist's wide shoe fits the plaster cast he made at the crime scene. It must be a perfect fit just as it was with Cinderella and the glass slipper. All the loose ends must be tied up to fit in with that shoe's style and width. Clues such as, wide shoes, distinct tread style, distribution of weight when the wearer walks, all of your subtle clues and red herrings must come together and prove to your reader without a shadow of doubt that this is our criminal.

As the sun melted all the snow and left no trace of footprints, the detective of your mystery story must melt/dissolve or point out all clues that follow in the direction of the antagonist. Everything must have stemmed from the original trail of footprints. The wide shoe is big enough to encompass all the reader and detective needs to know to solve the mystery. No surprise endings – no high heel shoe committed the crime when none was present in the whole story. A mystery must be honest with its readers or that writer will not be read again.

EXERCISES:

1.) Take a walk some place where you are bound to encounter footprints. Notice their similarities and differences. What do they tell you? Can you tell if the person or animal was running or walking? Heavy or light? Carrying something, dragging something? Write down all you can guess from the scene.

2.) Make up a story using the footprints you encountered as part of it.

QUOTES:

"Totally impossible to be well-dressed in cheap shoes." Hardy Amies, English Couturier

"Before you let the sun in, mind it wipes its shoes." Dylan Thomas, Welsh Poet

"I never saw them afterwards, or any sign of them, except three of their hats, one cap, and two shoes that were to fellows." Daniel Defoe, English Novelist & Journalist in Robinson Crusoe

Chapter Five

Wide Mouth Jars

"My task which I am trying to achieve is by the power of the written word to make you hear, to make you feel, it is before all, to make you see, that – and no more, and it is everything."

Joseph Conrad, Polish born English Novelist

When a person prepares to can or freeze produce from garden or market, they take certain steps. For our purposes, we will use a wide mouth jar because it is easier when you plan to use different sizes of produce. We are going to think of the ingredients in the process as the material for your story. It does not matter what kind of story you intend to write because what you need is the same for every story you write.

First, we must prepare our produce, fruits, or vegetables by peeling them. As with your story when you are preparing to write you must uncover what the story is about. You peel back the layers until you bare the fruit, vegetable, or in this case story line.

Secondly, you need to either prepare brine, syrup, or a dip to preserve the color and flavor of your produce. Something to marinate the produce until you are ready to cook it down. In the story, this process will be marinating the story in your mind. Letting it soak until you start to get a sense of what it is you want to tell.

Next, we must cut your produce into the proper size pieces. In the story, this is accomplished by dividing it into chapters. Here is where an outline comes in handy. It does not have to be the formal outline of your English class variety, but a simple chart that lets you know what chapters you need to tell your story.

Once this is done, we put all our ingredients into the pot to bring to a boil and cook to the desired state of doneness. Now you will add your sauce. In the story will it be the sugar of a romance, the tomato or other sauce of a mystery or the plain water of suspense with a tad of salt and other tangy spices. At this point, your story is to the peak of its readiness. You must keep it hot and bubbling as you ladle it into the wide mouth jars of the story container. The boiling action of the produce in the pot is the boiling forward movement of your plot. It must be kept at just the right boiling point so that the finished product will not spoil or fail to give the reader satisfaction of a good story. If you boil it too hard, it will all turn to mush, with no substance, no backbone. If you do not keep it at the perfect point between just at the boil and boiling, too hard your produce/story will be underdone/boring and not be satisfying to the reader.

When you have ladled all your story elements into the wide mouth jar of your story container, you must cap it to seal in all the freshness and juiciness of the story told at its proper time with all the proper ingredients, beginning, middle and ending.

Then you can put the produce/story away in a cool, dark place to age for a period. When you take it out, it will be sufficiently aged so that you get a fresh taste/perspective on the finished product. This is the time to begin to edit/rewrite/polish your story as if you were testing the produce to see if it has all the flavor you thought you had given it.

EXERCISES:

1.) Write a short story with these words somewhere in it: *greedy, seldom, Buddhist.*

2.) Pick the first sentence of a paragraph in a book you are reading and use it as your story starter.

QUOTES:

"Oh, a wondrous bird is the pelican!
His beak holds more than his belican.
He takes in his beak
Food enough for a week
But I'll be darned if I know how the helican."

Dixon Lanier Merrit, in the Nashville Banner,
22 April 1913

Chapter Six

Wide Screen Television

"Find ways to make your main character an integral part of the story, not merely an observer.

Heroes make things happen, they don't just let things happen to them."

Cynthia Whitcomb, Writer's Digest September 2001

A wide screen television makes everything appear life size. Vivid color makes you feel you are part of the action. The surround sound and volume control allows you to suit your mood, what type of show or event you are watching and how many people in the room need to hear what is going on. If you are sitting in a room quietly watching television alone or in another room doing something else while you listen – you adjust the volume to correspond

Your writing has to make your action, your story people life sized. You need to dress your scenes and people in vivid color to make them come alive. By vivid color, I do not necessarily mean what they are wearing. We need our characters to mimic real life in as much as we want our readers to empathize with their plight or their good fortune. We present them with characteristics, attitudes, likes and dislikes, style, mannerisms and everything and anything that will add Technicolor to our black and white story ideas.

Of course, you do not do a character sketch in the middle of your story for your reader; you sprinkle colorful tidbits of characterization and scene color through out your story. Think vibrant color for characters and places you want your readers to wake up to or remember. Think muted tones for your less important characters or schemes you do not want to give away all the clues to. A discerning reader will find them, but not necessarily everyone who is reading the story.

When you need to get a point across, turn up the volume to be sure your characters hear the background music of children's voices, dogs barking, thunder of an approaching storm or whatever music is playing.

When you watch a television show you can close your eyes and predict what type of scene is approaching, be it the dreamy strains foretelling of a love scene or eerie somber chords of disaster/action/adventure. The action – reaction needs to be heard in the reader's mind. You can use the same foreshadowing technique that music in a television show or movies create. By painting pictures with your words, you create the mood –tension in your story.

Sometimes when you read other writer's words, the pictures they paint flows across your unconscious mind like movies. You can see/hear/feel the scene and characters. They have turned up the volume – not the noise—just the volume with vivid descriptive nouns and verbs—may be the tiniest dash of adjective or adverbs. Usually their noun and verb choices arc strong enough that they do not need those helpers that tend to weaken prose rather than aid in meaning. Chains hung on strong nouns or verbs (the adjectives or adverbs) are like so much cheap costume jewelry.

As the introduction to any movie does, you should strive to set the stage for your story in such a way that you people it with life size characters who enter your vivid world of color that is coordinated with appropriate background music for your story. This can be done in your first few pages for some stories, for others it may take the first few chapters. Each chapter of our story demands the same careful consideration to create a moving tale of real life for your characters.

EXERCISES:

1.) Write a paragraph about an idea you have for a story. Do not use any adverbs or adjectives.

2.) Take a paragraph out of a book that you have been reading or recently read. Go through it and mark any adverbs or adjectives. Remove them from the story; does it make a difference in the meaning? Does it make the sentences stronger? If it does not make sense with out them can you add a new, stronger verb that can carry the sentence weight without using the adverb or adjective?

QUOTES:

"Music, when soft voices die,
Vibrates in the memory—
Odours, when sweet violets sicken,
Live within the sense they quicken"

Percy Bysshe Shelley, English Poet

Chapter Seven

Wide Berth

Letters with Tails Creating Flow

A wide interpretation
"God wove a web of loveliness
Of clouds and stars and birds.
But made not any thing at all
So beautiful as words."

Anna H. Branch, "Her Words"

Letters with tails like *y, g, j,* etc. relax your hand and your thinking as you go with a graceful flow of their shape.

Try it and see if the flow of them does not relax your tense wrist and hand. Perhaps by doing so it will loosen the tightness that threatens to cause a writer''s block in your cerebellum

The t's and i's interrupt your flow. They stop your thoughts to cross a *t* or dot an *i* as the case may be. For it is that millisecond that it takes for a thought or an idea to escape from the pen and float out to ether space never to be dreamed of the same way again in your lifetime.

Commas and periods also interrupt the flow of prose as it glides across the page. In my rough drafts I never use Commas or Periods but instead simple *~* marks because they do not seem to interrupt the flow of my thoughts as I pencil them on the page. It's a simple technique I learned from a Native American friend who never used traditional punctuation, but he wrote eloquently. Later when I do my revisions, I place appropriate punctuation where it is necessary. By then my idea is solidified and I can refine it without worrying about the interruption of t crossing or i dotting, punctuation takes a read and edit alone.

I still have not figured out a simple system to fix the flow of the dratted t or i words with out the lag in attention. There must be a substitute, perhaps a dash (–) could replace the t and a dot (.) could replace the i.

I could always write in shorthand, but some of that is even more confusing and flow stopping. Then I would have to translate the whole mess of chicken scratch (as my father called it) afterwards when I went to revise it. No, I think the simple dash and dot would work better and the squiggly ~ for the punctuation.

Here is what I think of the punctuation in my life:

Punctuation of the Self
Am I the word
The page
Or the message it serves

Perhaps nothing more than
Its punctuation

The comma pausing in life
The semi colon of illness
The dash in changes of direction

Before the final speck
The dot, the period
Of
Life lived.

By Billie Williams

EXERCISES:

1.) Write a paragraph you copy from a book you are reading substitute the tilde *~* for the punctuation. Then write a paragraph of the same number of lines but write only the letters *f, g, j, q, y, z.*

2.)In another paragraph, tell how writing a paragraph of the loopy letters made you feel. Did it relax your hand ~ your mood?

QUOTES:

"Another sport which wastes unlimited time is comma-hunting. Once start a comma and the whole pack will be off, full cry, especially if they have had literary training...But comma-hunting is so exciting as to be a little dangerous. There is some fear that the conduct of business being properly obstructed on its demerits."
Francis M Cornford, English Academic

Chapter Eight

Double-wide

"Mid pleasures and palaces though we may roam,
Be it ever so humble, there is no place like home."

J.H. Payne, American actor, Dramatist, & Songwriter

A doublewide trailer home is not two houses but one holding more. Like a novel rather than a short story. The doublewide is portable, still a mobile home, as the novel is still a story. In a short story, you have beginning, middle, and end just as in a novel. Portability means you can cover a lot of territory with your short story in a little space, but a novel allows you to explore a double wide – larger picture.

As your doublewide is delivered in halves to your land and your novel is delivered in halves. The first half leads you up to the peak – the major turning point of your story, which may or may not necessarily, be the climax. At the very least, it will be the major point of your story, the reason, and the motivating factor of your story. The second half leads from the peak action, point/climax to the dénouement and the end.

The doublewide has most of its plumbing on one side of the house. There is a good reason for this. This is to lessen the stress on the plumbing fixtures and pipes but also the necessity of another connection, which could be the source of a leak. Your story should contain a good deal of back-story and introductory business in the beginning sections to facilitate the putting together of the story idea without leaks about the climax leads, but not leaks.

The furnace is contained on one side of the house, but the ductwork must run, below through out the entire doublewide structure. This ductwork is the labyrinth of clues and foreshadowing you wish to construct throughout the underlying framework of your story.

While your doublewide trailer was transported to your site, the windows and doors were locked to prevent damage. Your windows were also covered to prevent breakage. In this state, there is no entrance to the home. No peeking is allowed into the interior to see the layout, or the color of the walls, carpeting, or cabinetry. You have to rely on the descriptive brochure for the details. Your novel/story must present enough information to give some idea of what to expect once we are allowed inside the doublewide novel.

Your doublewide could be delivered to a concrete slab or a full basement. The choice is yours. The novel or story you deliver makes a similar choice. You have prepared us before hand to see that the story/house is finished when it is set on the concrete slab or else there is another level to your story/novel we have not explored. The moving and setting in place of the doublewide on the basement then becomes the anti-climax. The underlying basement houses the climax, which you will lead us through once your doublewide is set in place and the roof is seamlessly, connected.

Once you have given us the climax -the basement – there remains some clean up and final setting up of the house. That is, tying up loose ends of the story so that all the characters, all the questions raised, and all the events are wrapped and neatly packaged into a complete story housed between two artfully done, doublewide covers.

EXERCISES: 1.) Rough sketch a house outline on a piece of paper. Put your story parts and a brief summary of each in the various spots of the house as discussed in the above article. Perhaps you begin in the attic with a scrapbook of back-story. On the other hand, maybe you choose to start in the first floor kitchen area with present day drama. You decide, it is your house, your doublewide novel. How many rooms will you have? Three rooms are essential remember, the beginning, middle and end. Now WRITE!

QUOTE:

"Home is the place where when you have to go there, they have to take you in." Robert Frost, American Poet.

"Direct your eyesight inward and you will find
A thousand regions to our mind
Yet undiscovered. Travel them, and be
Expert in home cosmography."

William Habington, English Poet.

Chapter Nine

Wide- Open

"As an experience, madness is terrific...And in its lava, I still find most of the things I write about." Virginia Woolf, English Novelist

That could be wide-open spaces, wide open as in racing a Ferrari spots car, or a ship captain's command, full speed ahead. It is important when you do your first draft of your story that you approach it with your mind wide open and fully engaged in the task. Do not stop yourself to let the critic fix sentence structure, grammar, or any of the mechanics.

Allow yourself and your imagination free rein. Get your words down on paper while the lava in your story volcano is hot and flowing. If you stop to let the cold north wind of criticism cool the lava flow, your passion will evaporate from your story. You will notice if you are reading some of your own writings, your best pieces are full of emotion-backed flow, a red-hot lava flow, a passion that sings out in vivid prose.

Along with the wide-open flow, a wide-open imagination is essential. Opening your mind to your imagination is as simple as brainstorming, clustering, listing or mapping. *(See below for an explanation of these terms if you are not familiar with them.) What these techniques do is allow you to think wide...reaching for all possible connections. The lava flow seeks every crevasse, every depression or hole so to does your imagination if you allow it to flow far and wide.

If you have never read *The Phantom Tollbooth*, by Norton Juster, or one of the Amelia Bedelia books, I would highly recommend that you do. These books show you what spice imagination can add to your story. The lava flow of your imagination sparked story can light little fires that burn away from the lava path and may provide interesting depth, back story, flashbacks etc. to your main story. On the other hand, may send you on a journey you never imagined.

When a volcano explodes, the lava flow is a bright orange/red glow, which signifies the heat of the molten rock. The heated rock flows freely; slowly as it gets away from the source of the heat, it cools, ceases to flow and hardens into another shape and size from its original self. Your idea once incubated until it becomes molten and ready to explode from you in a passionate orange/red flow onto the page, becomes a new or different entity just like the volcanic rock. You shape it while it is still orange/red. You let it cool and while it's still malleable, you edit it. Then you let it cool all the way.

Set it aside for a few days, a week or longer until the ink dries and your thoughts settle down.

Later after the lava has cooled the parched earth sends up shoots of green – renewed growth from beneath the hardened rock. When you look again at your story with fresh eyes – you may see the growth of ideas that need to be added to make the story whole, or things that need to be clarified.

The story is all there it just needs nurturing and pruning to give it fresh, invigorating growth, as you prepare it to send out. You have done your market study; you cleaned up your story until it is as highly polished as it can be. Now send it out, some editor has been waiting for a fresh volcanic eruption to wake up his publication.

EXERCISES:

Take out a story you have put away for some time. Or go back through your journals (You are keeping a journal aren't you? If not, why not? However, that will be discussed elsewhere.) Re-read what you have written with fresh eyes. Revise it now that you have distanced yourself from it.

*Brainstorming: Write the word you want to brainstorm at the top of your page. Then let other words, phrases, and parts of ideas flow onto the page as they come into your mind. If you have a partner you can come up with more ideas, but you can do it alone to. Do not discount any idea you have—go deep do this at least until you feel you have exhausted any possible ideas.

Clustering: You write your word in the center of the page and circle it. Then you draw lines from that word and write other words that come to mind because of that word. Circle each of them as you do them. If those words spark words, draw lines from them, write the related word, and circle it. Keep going until you are sure you have exhausted your ideas.

Listing: Is just that. Write your word at the top of the page and list every word you can think of that goes with it.

Mapping: Is similar to all of the above. It takes you from your original idea or word to all the possible avenues of thought that can be connected to it.

QUOTES:

"I by no means rank poetry high in the scale of intelligence—this may look like affection—but it is my real opinion—it is the lava of the imagination whose eruption prevents an earthquake." Lord Byron, English Poet

"Old religious factions are volcanoes burnt out." Edmund Burke, Irish born Whig politician & Man of Letters

Chapter Ten

The Wide Gray Elephant Leg

"Different persons growing up in the same language are like different bushes trimmed and trained to take the shape of identical elephants. The anatomical details of twigs and branches will fulfill the elephantine shape differently from bush to bush, but the overall outward results are alike."

W.V.O. Quine, American Philosopher.

Thinking of things that are wide, I picture a wide gray elephant's leg, which reminds me of the story about the three blind men. Each man focused on some different aspect of the whole elephant. None of them knew the whole creature was an elephant and neither knew what the other was feeling. From the descriptions, they could have all been talking about some totally different object.

To one blind, man the broad leg and foot of the elephant felt like a tree trunk. Let us pretend that the blind man is an author. The author has just described a broad/wide rough feeling object that is stationary and cannot be lifted from the ground. The rough texture could resemble bark; the size could indicate tree. Indeed, anyone

45

could make that assumption if the author did not explain clearly, what it is s/he is showing the reader. If the skin had a rough texture; if the animals skin, or if the animals skin on his leg reminded one of...the four different versions paint a totally different picture of the same thing in the mind.

The second blind man/author feels the thin tail and it becomes a rope. That again could be a logical assumption. Close your eyes and think about a good horsehair or hemp rope.

The rope is thinnish, but not too thin. Rough, but not too rough. Perhaps it is raveled on one end, but not too raveled. To a child, this could become an elephant tail as he tucks it into the waistband at the back of his pants; or, it could be a rope that he will use to pull an imaginary trailer. It is up to the author to lead the reader to his conclusion. Left to his devices the water puddle could be a pool of blood, or the edge of a lake or even an ocean. The writer can use this to his advantage in a mystery by leading the reader astray, red herring, they call that. It is to the author's advantage to provide a good, clear description of what it is he wants his reader to see. Keep your reader tethered to your belt with the description that fills his mind with huge gray elephants.

The third blind man/author felt the elephant's trunk and immediately became terrified. Can you imagine the alarm he would feel if a Boa Constrictor —or a Python appeared in his mind? How would a blind man cope with a deadly snake? As a writer, you could place him in the snake's death grip or save him just in time; or you could let the elephant spew water, bellow, and give him away.

Description keeps your reader focused on the picture you want him to see, keeping him grounded so to speak. This description must be brief and evocative. It must be given while moving your story forward. It is necessary to ground your reader, but without the forward movement, the story would become static and boring. You must work for balance here, as with your narration or your dialog. It is necessary to give your reader place, time, and mood but you cannot let it bog down your story. Your big gray elephant with broad cylinder like legs, enormous body, tail that reminds you of a heavy hemp rope, must be moving through your story toward some purpose.

Perhaps the great gray elephant thundered into the clearing, ears fanning the air, trunk like a huge boa constrictor raised as he trumpeted his warning. Can you see this huge freight train bearing down on you? You no longer see a tree standing motionless or hemp rope dangling lifeless in space. Your story image is charging head long into the sights of your elephant gun/and or your reader's mind.

Choose your words to paint the picture you want your reader to see in ways that make it live in the reader's mind. Be sure your reader winds up on the same page with you when you tell a story about something big, do not leave him imagining a tree where an elephant is standing.

EXERCISES:

1.) Read one of the Amelia Bedelia books. Then write an explanation of your favorite animal to tell a blind person what it looks like.

2.)Picture a shadow on a wall; describe that shadow so that a person on the other end of the telephone will know what you are describing.

QUOTES:

"Words are cheap. The biggest thing you can say is 'elephant'." Charles Chaplin, English film actor, director speaking on the universality of silent films.

"Nature's great master piece, than elephant,
The only harmless great thing." John Donne, English Poet

Chapter Eleven

Wide-Leaf Plant

"I come from a backward place, your duty is supplied by life around you. One guy plants bananas; another plants cocoa; I am a writer, I plant lines. There''s the same clarity of occupation, and the sense of devotion."

Derek Walcott, West Indian Poet and Dramatist

Imagining your novel story as a wide (broad) leaf plant such as the colorful Croton, a native of Hawaii, we will compare it and the parts of a story novel. This plant is a hardy plant for office or home. Think of the plant in its totality and its environment. The Croton itself consists of roots, woody stem, leaves and veins that run visibly through those leaves. It is in a pot full of rich organic soil to which we have probably added some additional fertilizer.

Writing a novel is similar to this broad-leafed plant. The roots of your plant/novel are grounded in a rich soil of ideas. Your thesis statement, your plot or synopsis, grows from these roots. Your roots have to be large enough to support your plant/novel. The larger your idea – root system, the more branches and leaves your plant will be able to support. There are some things your broad leaf

49

plant and novel need to sustain life. As a plant needs soil, fertilizer, water, and sunlight, the same ingredients will nourish and support your novel story ideas.

First, you need to see to the proper nourishment – feeding of your plant and novel story. The ingredients for a healthy plant and novel are the same. Rich organic soil/ideas that fertilize complications, challenges, confrontations, and conflict to feed your story.

Secondly, life-giving water is essential to sustain the life of the plant. The water of your novel will be the narration, dialogue and characterization that moves through out your novel pushing, pulling, guiding your characters up through the network of veins feeding your chapters (leaves) and your (plant) story.

To this mix of food and water, we need to add a little sunlight enough to give our leaves (chapters) what they need to create oxygen and put it out into the air of your story atmosphere, enough so, it can synthesize the color and livelihood of the entire plant/novel story. The light you shine into the dark corners illuminate your characters, bring them and their conflict or novel problems out where the reader becomes engulfed in the life of them.

The little nubs along the stem of your plant/novel story are possible plot points. These are where a new shoot could develop into a full sub-plot of your story. The stem of the wide-leaf is your means of connecting to the whole; the idea imbedded in the fertile idea soil of your novel.

Think of the veins of a Croton leaf. They are a different color than the leaf and are vividly evident. These veins run off at different intervals from the main vein. Think of these leaves as your chapters. The main vein is the path from the core/stem of the idea of your chapter that carries the theme throughout the chapter. The various veins going to the edge of the leaf are the story threads that flow through the chapter. They always connect to the main idea stem. They are contained in a certain shape and size, as are most chapters; your reader has come to expect certain things in each chapter of your novel. According to, and because of the rules of the genre, you are writing.

Each chapter has a beginning, middle, and an end. The end usually is a hook to catch your reader and drag him/her to the next chapter. The chapters, like the leaves, have a basic shape with similar veins through chapter after chapter.

Closer to the tip of the plant or the climax of your story novel, your chapters will hold more life in less space creating the pressure that will catapult your climax. As with the plant, the smallest leaf at the top of the plant still has all the characteristics of the first leaf, but it is condensed, ready to force that drop of life sustaining sap from the tip of that new leaf. Once released, your climax and the drop of sap slowly evaporate while some of it slides back down the plant to nourish the new leaf. This drop of sap is the life of your novel. The climax forces that last bit of life to the top and out falling back on itself. It nourishes the story by cleaning up all loose ends. The evaporation of the tension, the dénouement, is the final chapter in the development of your last leaf/chapter and the end of your novel story.

Plant your story in the fertile soil of ideas, attend to its basic needs and your results will be a vigorous healthy story that blooms profusely where you planted it.

EXERCISES:

1.) Sketch a basic plant shape, with roots, stem, and leaves. Put veins in the leaves. Put fertile soil around its roots. Now, brainstorm a story idea and fill in the various appropriate places on your plant diagram.

2.) Write a story about how you would introduce a new plant into your garden. Relate that to writing. How is it the same? How is it different?

QUOTES:

"What is a weed? A plant whose virtues have not been discovered." Ralph Waldo Emerson, American Philosopher & Poet

"Fame is no plant that grows on mortal soil." John Milton, English Poet

Chapter Twelve

Wide Shadows

"We walked up to the house and stood some minutes watching the swallows that flew about restlessly, and flung their shadows upon the sunbright walls of the old building, the shadows glanced and twinkled, interchanged and crossed each other expanded and shrunk up, appeared and disappeared every instant."

Dorothy Wordsworth, English Writer

Shadows depend on time of day, intensity of light whether it is sun light or an artificial light source, and the direction from which it comes. When you write, you choose how your shadows will play with your prose by setting your light sources as well as its direction. Think of your point of view as the light source. You have four choices here that each has certain advantages and disadvantages.

Noonday shadows stay close to the object much like expository writing that expresses itself concisely, keeping close to one particular subject at all times. The author stays close to the subject leaving little room for a shadow to wander. Noonday sun is first person singular point of view. It is the "I" viewpoint; it is the noonday sun's shadow. This person cannot see into other characters shadows. He cannot stray far from himself. What he sees, feels, or hears. He brings the reader closer to the story and is more like the way we live our lives. The advantages of this viewpoint are: it gives the reader a sense of connection to the story; the reader experiences the intensity of a personal story; it can create a close up portrait of the character; and a variety of moods can be created by the point of view character's thoughts, feelings, and actions.

There are also some disadvantages to this point of view. It is very limited. The character cannot hear, feel, or see what the other characters are thinking or doing outside of his immediate physical space. Perhaps the closeness to the story also limits his perception of the whole picture. Sometimes it is helpful to know what the other characters are going through to enrich the story.

Early morning shadows chase through the landscape quickly as an action/thriller type story does. The third person omniscient point of view gives the author license to be with other characters thoughts and deeds no matter who is the lead character. The author knows everything that is going on in the story. He can get into everyone's head. He has a broader perspective to tell the story and he can play one character's feelings against another's. Care must be taken here to make it easy for your reader to decide who is speaking or acting. A rule of thumb is never to change characters in the same paragraph. It would be better to change chapters – or time – or location before switching from one characters point of view to another rather than risk loosing your reader. The disadvantages of this point of view are that you may dilute the reader's identity with anyone in the story. It is too easy for the reader to become confused about who feels what. You could also lose the intrinsic emotion of the story that the single point of view would give the reader. In addition, in this point of view it is easy for readers to lose focus on the heart of the story you are presenting. I would advise you to be cautious when choosing the busy, scurrying morning shadows that play on our manuscript while the day (or in this case the story) is busy deciding what it will be.

Lazy afternoon shadows meander in and out, and around while clinging steadfastly to the source of light. Third person singular is the perfect choice for the long lazy afternoon shadows. The reader still identifies with one character, but using one voice for the protagonist or main character and another for the narrator expands the view. Each can comment on events. This gives a broader over view to the story but still keeps your reader tucked in close to the shadow of your story. The disadvantage of this viewpoint is it is still limited to one character and you need to balance between the character and the narrator so that one does not out voice or over power the other.

The artificial light of the night creates new images out of familiar objects. These are the horror stories of such authors as Dean Koontz, Douglas Clegg, or Ann Rice. The voice you chose for these is limited only by what you want to show your reader. Pull him in close in the first person singular as Stephen King does in *Misery*, or distance you and the reader as Douglas Clegg does in *Infinity*.

You still have one other choice you can use for your point of view character – that is usually used for how-to manuals or sometimes effectively in young adult stories where the creators let the reader choose how the story will go by supplying various directions and endings. This is the second person point of view—the you. It gives the reader a sense that the book is written just for him or her.

Shadows and light dance, scurry, or stand very still in the noonday sun. The intricate weavings of the street light shadows have sparked many a sleepless night. Your writing, whatever shadow you choose, can influence the reader long into many sunlit days and moonless nights. Play with point of view. Rewrite paragraphs to see how they sound from other povs and perhaps you will discover you were shinning the light from the wrong source or the wrong direction.

EXERCISE: .

1.) Pick a story you have been reading and choose a paragraph, rewrite it from a different point of view. Notice how it changes the story. Did the author pick the right voice or do you think a different point of view works better?

2.) Examine one of your pieces. Try changing point of view several times. Which gives the reader the most satisfaction? Which pulls the reader in to participate in the story?

QUOTES:

"The shadows now so long do grow,
That brambles like tall cedars show,
Molehills seem mountains, and the ant
Appears a monstrous elephant."

Charles Cotton, English Poet

"When the sun sets, shadows, that showed at noon but small, appear most long and terrible." Nathaniel Lee, English Dramatist

"I have a little shadow that goes in and out with me,
And what can be the use of him is more than I can see.
He is very, very like me from the heels up to the head;
And I see him jump before me, when I jump into my bed."

Robert Louis Stevenson, Scottish novelist

Chapter Thirteen

Wide Receiver

"The great fallacy is that the game is first and last about winning. It is nothing of the kind. The game is about glory, it is about doing things in style and with a flourish, about going out and beating the lot, not waiting for them to die of boredom."

Danny Blanchflower, English football player

PLAYERS

Ball — Synopsis

Quarterback —The Writer

Wide Receiver —- Editor

Team — Idea generating, creating, researching, writing, re-writing, editing, and formatting

Opposing Team — Bad grammar, typos, weak or dull plot, shallow characters, unsatisfactory resolutions

You have finished your novel, polished it until it shines. Think of yourself as the quarter back in a foot ball game. Football in hand you have searched the field (market analysis) for a wide receiver (editor) to pass your novel to. Your wide receiver will be your chosen editor. Are you sure, the ball has enough air in it? That the strings aren't coming undone? You need a good ball, properly inflated to be able to hit the receiver you have targeted.

There is a whole team of muscle waiting to sack the quarterback and crush the receiver so that the two never connect. Let us look at the synopsis. It needs enough air – conflict, character development and action to fill the pigskin (novel) full enough. Air is in the present tense otherwise it is carbon dioxide; your synopsis must also be present tense.

Is the hide on the ball tough enough or in this case is your plot strong enough to carry the book? An editor will be asking this question as he reads your synopsis. Some other things he may be asking are will your conflict, the way you have written it, hold the reader? Are your ending, resolution/completed pass, satisfying enough for the reader/fans in the stands? Your conclusion should flow naturally from the conflict in your story, a perfect pass. Did you give the quarterback enough muscle and hand-eye coordination to throw the ball straight over the heads of those would be blockers?

You need to give your editor the story plot briefly. Your quarterback does not want to be sacked. He does not have a lot of time. In a nutshell, tell him the major conflict, introduce your hero or heroine by telling their goals (motivation) and what achieving those goals means to them (motives). You must also include any internal or external conflicts the characters have going on that will have a bearing on your story. You should include key scenes that illuminate plot twists, reversals or set backs that lead to what we call the "dark moment," where things can't possibly get any worse. You need to pump this air into the ball and add the resolution.

It is never a good idea to leave the ending off. Those strings all need to be tied. That is the place where the quarterback targets his grip to ensure an accurate pass to the wide receiver. Think of your editor as your confessor, your wide receiver… he needs to know it all. He needs the whole ball. Only a part of it will not result in a touch down or in this case a sale for your book. Concentrate on getting your key scenes, the heart of your story, into the ball game.

That is the goal of the quarterback and the wide receiver – the whole team. All the effort, writing, researching, re-writing, self-editing the whole team is the effort you expended to get this far. Do not let your team down by fumbling the ball, or missing the wide receiver now, by not doing a comprehensive synopsis. The quarterback only has one chance to hit his mark once the ball leaves his grasp. Sure, you can always send it out again if it is rejected, but why not sharpen your aim and pack that pigskin, protect that quarterback, and give the receiver everything he needs to go for the touch down.

EXERCISES:

1.) Get a copy of the condensed Reader's Digest books. Pick one story. Find the book in your library, read, and compare the two. What is missing? Does the Reader's Digest version still have all the essentials a synopsis might need?

2.) Take another book that you like and are familiar with see if you can write a synopsis of the book. What did this author give the editor to make him want to buy this manuscript? What are the key scenes in this book? (If you would rather you can use a magazine story or a short story from somewhere else. They all need the same ingredients no matter what the length.)

QUOTES:

*"For when the One Great Scorer comes to mark against your name, **h**e writes, not that you won or lost—but how you played the game."*

Grantland Rice, American Sports Writer

"Football? It's the beautiful game."

Pele, Brazilian football player

"The analytical engine weaves algebraic patterns just as the Jacquard loom weaves flowers and leaves." Ada Lovelace, English Mathematician, daughter of Lord Byron.

Chapter Fourteen

Writing Wide

Corralling the Stallion

(Reining in the Wild Stallion of your writing)

*"He understood...Walt Whitman who laid end to end words
never seen in each other's company before outside of a dictionary,
and Herman Melville who split the atom of the traditional novel in
the effort to make whaling a universal metaphor."*

David Lodge, English Novelist

1. Lazy Old Nags and Wimpy Verbs

An old nag of a horse does not get much appreciation. He or
she is slow, plodding, and not capable of carrying a full load.
Wimpy verbs like felt, feel, thought, and think, are like the
plodding old nag, they cannot carry a vivid image. Verbs must
convey a very specific thought, emotion or action—that is what
verbs do. When you are looking for wimpy verbs, remove the
modifiers to check for the strength of your verb. Example: The
deer was snorting – remove the verb modifier – snorting and you

have "The deer was." The sentence reworked should read – The deer snorted. It still gives the image/picture of what the deer looks and sounds like, but in the present tense, giving your story immediacy or action.

Occasionally, you need the old nag to give a green horn or a child a safe easy ride. Occasionally, you may need to have a "to be" verb followed by a modifier, because you do not want your writing to sound stilted, wordy, or pretentious. Sometimes it is the best way to state what you need to say, but remember to look at rewrite possibilities for your sentences using strong verbs instead of the week "to be" variations.

2. Locoweed and Prepositions

If a horse gets into locoweed it does what the weed implies – makes him crazy confused and disoriented. If left unchecked he will drink water until he literally drowns himself in it.

Prepositions can make your writing confusing. They can stop the flow of the story you are trying to tell. The prepositions are the "over, in, under of "over the hill", "in the house," "under the weather." Did you notice the double error? Not only the preposition "under" is used but also the cliché that contained it. Usually by omitting the preposition, the sentence automatically gains strength. Thinking "out of the box," becomes creative thinking. For instance: Jane went in the house. Compared with Jane entered the house through the front door. – Gives us more information and shows us where Jane is. Jane is not a ghost who walks in the house – she uses the front door. No locoweed no confusion.

3. Draft horses and Adverbs

You will never plump up weak verbs by adding more weight with the overworked ""ly" words. Some adverbs can enliven your work. However, for your prose to be effective you must put it on an adverb diet and use them sparingly. Rather like eating a piece of chocolate cake that hits the spot or tastes satisfying. Would you really get any pleasure out of eating a whole chocolate cake with chocolate frosting? Okay, so initially, it may make you feel pampered, but what about the over stuffed feeling, the feeling of guilt, the added pants size, would you really want to eat a whole cake at one sitting?

An over weight horse cannot do the work of a sinewy steed. As with your adverbs, one piece is better than excess with the whole. Try this example: She ate rapidly OR she gulped her food. He vacuumed his food. The second and third sentences give you a picture of just how fast the person is eating where rapidly could mean many things to different people.

A draft horse is big and meant for work. Your sentences should be big with clarity and sharp active verbs.

4. Clichés are rather like an appaloosa horse.

All those spots but only on his back half make him the, excuse the pun, "butt end of a lot of jokes." As with clichés which are to be avoided because they give your writing an apologetic feel. As though you were too lazy to look for a precise or exact word to fit the definition or point you wanted to make. Like the appaloosa's spots, they are all over half of him making him a spotted horse but not really. To one person the appaloosa horse would be spotted to another he would be a mixed up breed of a horse. We use cliché's because they are so easy. They are the coward's way out. You need to use your creativity to come up with a better way to say the same thing. Cliché's became cliché's because they conveyed their ideas or sentiments so precisely. They became like commercial jingles, the first thing that pops into your head when you need to describe something. Your writing will stand out if you invent a new way of saying the same thing without dragging that overworked lazy-man's-way-out cliché's into your prose. Let the mother wonder if that is appaloosa foal, a paint, or pinto meandering away from her.

5. Redundancy – twins born in the horse world are rare.

In your prose redundancies should never occur. Repeating information should tell you that you have not given your reader an accurate and true description the first time. If you have to repeat a description, an incident's explanation, or dialog even if you use a different set of words, it still means you did not do the job the first time and it's time to rework your story to reflect what you really meant to say. Rewording, the same message, to repeat it, insults your reader's intelligence. Repeated information is not the only way that redundancies occur. Sometimes we use combinations of words that are redundant. These words add weight but not meaning to your work. Think of the use of sit down or stand up. You know that if you sit – you are placing your bottom on chair or something similar at the very least you are going down to do it. You cannot sit standing. Which brings us to stand up – can you stand down? I guess you could stand down wind but that is a whole other idea. Some redundancies are laughable in their quirkiness, comedians use these to their advantage, and you should not if you want your readers to take you seriously. Read your prose to look for these twin horses before someone spots them and no longer takes your prose earnestly.

6. All spotted horses are not Pinto's, but all Pinto's are spotted. A spotted horse looks like he was caught in a paint fight.

Similes and metaphors can be creative if they enhance the imagery of your story. A simile compares two unlike things. Similes easily become clichés. A metaphor claims one thing IS something else. Metaphors are less likely to be abused because they are more direct. A clumsy or inappropriate metaphor can weaken or destroy your story.

Simile: Pinto horse looks like a beagle dog with his splotches of color.

Metaphor: A Pinto horse IS the beagle of the horse family.

The writer must always be sure that the tone of the simile or metaphor matches the type of story he is telling. A humorous comparison in the form of a simile or metaphor would have an ill effect in a horror/suspense/thriller plot. Unless, your intent is deliberate with the intention of lifting the mood of the terror or tension you have created for your reader. That usually is not the case.

Then too always be alert for the mixed metaphor or simile. One type of reference in juxtaposition with another causes a mixed metaphor. For example, In "Woe Is I", Patricia T. O'Conner uses the phrase "volley of abuse" as a hail of bullets raining down on some one. The same phrase used as, "the volley of abuse was the straw that broke the camel's back" is a mixed metaphor. We have volley –meaning fusillade of bullets and straw – there is no similarity there. The competing images drown each other out, she says. She illustrates with several more: "The silver lining at the end of the tunnel' or, "Don't count your chickens until the cows come home." Good for a laugh but certainly will not do your story any good. It is usually more desirable for you to find a more creative or original way to say something than to use an "old horse that has been ridden hard and put away wet." How often have you seen or heard that phrase used? Cliché you say? Pasha!

When you begin to memorize or at least engrain the six ugly nags in your memory bank you will see them "cropping up" everywhere. It is up to you to cut them ruthlessly from the herd of your story corral in order that you use only the most virile steeds, which will result in writing tight, eclectic prose.

EXERCISES:

1. Take a story you have been working on and ruthlessly pare out any wimpy verbs. Take them all out. Then go back through and make your story stronger. Change the verb to a stronger verb form whenever you can. Use a dictionary of synonyms or thesauruses to find better choices if you need to. At the same time, check for adverbs that may be adding word count but not meaning to your story.

2.Look through one of your stories for similes. Can you restate the same sentence using stronger words? Weed out redundancies while you look for similes.

QUOTES:

""*Know the Atman (the spirit, the self; smaller than the smallest atom, greater than the vast spaces) as Lord of a chariot, and the body as the chariot itself. Know that reason is the charioteer; and the mind indeed is the reins. The horses they say are the senses; and their paths are the objects of sense."* The Upanishads, Hindu sacred treatises

"The man who is born in a stable is not a horse." Proverbs

"A fly, sir, may sting a stately horse and make him wince; but one is but an insect, and the other is a horse still" Samuel Johnson, English Poet, Critic and Lexicographer

"The tygers of wrath are wiser than the horses of instruction." William Blake, English Poet

Billie A Williams

Billie A. Williams is an author of fiction, non-fiction and Poetry. Her first novel ""Death by Candlelight," was published in October 2002 by Wings ePress, Inc. (available at) www.wings-press.com

She has published non-fiction in Thema Magazine, Guide magazine for Children, Novel Advice.com, Blueberry Press Write Now, and various publications online and in print. Her articles, columns and feature stories have appeared in newspapers in Wisconsin, Michigan and Colorado. Short stories have been published in Flash Fiction, Mystery Time, Wake Up Writing, Word Mage.com, Great Write Shark.com and Red Writing Hood.

Her poetry has been published in anthologies and print publications such as True Love Magazine.

Ms. Williams also has published book reviews for Ebooks N Bytes, Patricia Lewin, Story Lady, Writing Etc. and other online publications.

She is a contributing editor for Novel Advice, and Blue Berry Press.

She's a member of:

Wisconsin Regional Writer's Association

National Association of Women Writer's

69

Sister's In Crime

Women in the Arts

Society of Children's Book Writers & Illustrators

She lives with her husband in a small rural Wisconsin community where the winters are long and cold and the people are warm and friendly.

Visit her web site at www.billiewilliams.com

Email her at wordcrafter123@hotmail.com

Also by Billie Williams

Death by Candlelight

Family dynamics have a far reaching affect. Wealth such as that of Randolph Ord III and poverty like that of his wife, Danielle's family show no favorites when a unit ceases to function.

Danielle Ord watched her parents play out their roles in an abusive marriage; she exists in a relationship fueled by alcohol and drug abuse which began as rebellion. The abused wife is ready to resort to an elaborate scheme and at the same time Ruth Ord, the sister, has her own designs. When the two women's paths cross, their plans are altered. But Randolph Ord III still turns up dead

It is now up to detective Sandy Marsh to find the real killer. Is his judgment being compromised by the growing attraction he feels toward the newly widowed Danielle Ord? Both women have motive and opportunity; but a third figure emerges with ties to organized crime

Death by Candlelight is available at

www.wings-press.com/

More Great Writing Books

Writing Wide: Exercises in Creative Writing by Billie A. Williams

Jumpstart Your Writing Career and Snag Paying Assignments by Beth Ann Erickson

Bob Bly's Guide to Freelance Writing Success: How to Make $100,000 A Year As A Writer And Have The Time Of Your Life Doing it by Robert W. Bly

Weekly Writes: 52 Weeks of Writing Bliss! by Shery Ma Belle Arrieta

Grass Roots Book Marketing: Almost 300 Free Ways to Sell Your E-books and PODs by Rusty Fischer

Pump Up Your Prose for Publication, Profits, and Prestige by Shaunna Privratsky

365 Tips for Writers: Inspiration, Writing Prompts, and Beat The Block Tips to Turbo Charge Your Creativity by Dawn Colclasure

You can purchase any of these fantastic titles at your local bookstore, online bookstore or publisher direct at FilbertPublishing.com

Printed in the United States
118087LV00002B/2/A